DREAMY DESSERTS

DREAMY
DESSERTS

Rosemary Butler

Sun on Earth™ Books
Heathsville, Virginia

Published by Sun on Earth™ Books

www.sunonearth.com

Illustrations by the author.

Publisher's Cataloging-in-Publication Data
Butler, Rosemary.
    Dreamy Desserts / Rosemary Butler.— Ist ed.
        p. cm.
    ISBN: 978-1-883378-25-7
            1. Foods—Poetry.
            I. Title.

    PS430. B88. D7436 2023
    811'.6—dc23

    ISBN: 978-1-883378-25-7

Life is uncertain. Eat dessert first.

— Ernestine Ulmer

APPLE

PANDOWDY

APPLE PANDOWDY

Days can be sunny
Or days can be cloudy.
But any day is
A day for Pandowdy.

Served in a bowl,
Or even in glasses,
Sweetened with sugar,
And also molasses.

Adored by pandas,
Who like dishes sweet.
Apple Pandowdy's
Their favorite treat.

ARM of THE Gypsy

ARM OF THE GYPSY

Arm of the Gypsy,
A fabulous cake,
For breakfast, with coffee.
To keep you awake.

Or maybe at teatime
Would also be nice.
Then, I will cut you
A generous slice.

BAKED
ALASKA

BAKED ALASKA

I plan to see a polar bear
And think that I will ask her:
Please tell me how you always make
A perfect Baked Alaska.

It takes you years and years to learn,
Baked Alaska's hard to make.
To keep ice cream frozen in the cake
And not become a lake.

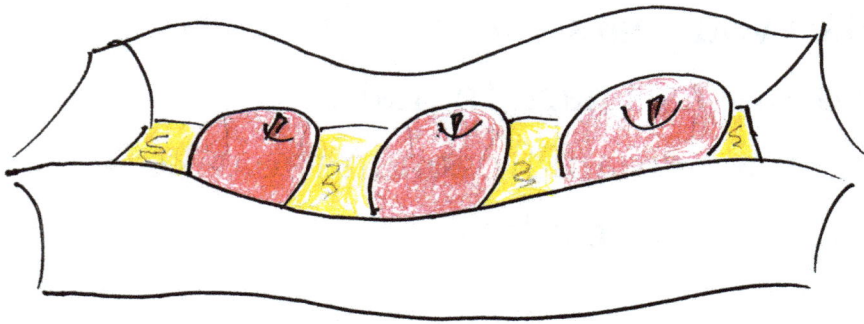

BAKED

APPLES

BAKED APPLES

Brown sugar-baked apples
Announce that it's fall.
Without them, the fall
Would be no fun at all!

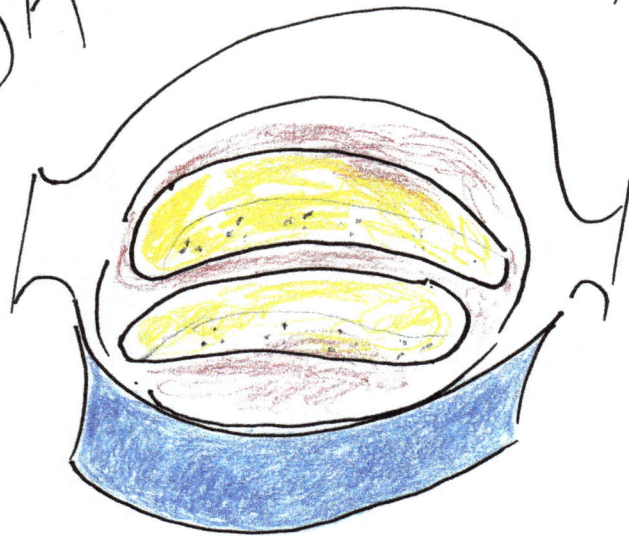

BANANAS FOSTER

BANANAS FOSTER

On the list of great desserts,
High up on the roster,
Is a favorite, far and wide,
It's called "Bananas Foster."

This luscious treat was dreamed up by
A Richard Foster, just in time
For his promotion to be the new
New Orleans Commissioner of Crime!

How could this ordinary man
Create this great sensation,
Of bananas, butter,
Brown sugar, rum,
A stunning innovation!

BERRY
CHERRY
COBBLER

BERRY CHERRY COBBLER

A merry cobbler
Makes beautiful shoes.
A berry cobbler
Makes ohs! and makes oohs!

BERRY

COMPOTE

BERRY COMPOTE

Please join me tonight
For a dinner divine,
In which every course comes
With the very best wine.

The last course is splendid,
A Berry Compote.
This dazzling dessert
Wins my blue-ribbon vote.

BLUEBERRY PIE

BLUEBERRY PIE

Why would Blueberry Pie make you feel blue?
Blue has meant sad. We know this is true.
But you'll never feel blue around Blueberry Pie.
Blue's the color of sea and the color of sky.

It's the Grotto that's Blue by the Isle of Capri.
It's the river that flows by the state, Tennessee.
It's the inlet that once was the wet Zuider Zee.

So don't ever cry over Blueberry Pie.
Be happy, not sad. Think of clouds in the sky.

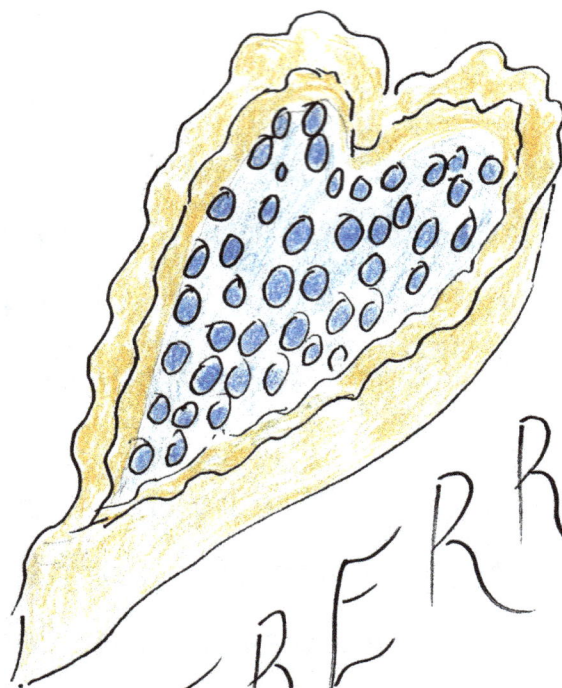

BLUEBERRY
TART

BLUEBERRY TART

Blueberry Tart, Blueberry Tart,
Especially a tart in the shape of a heart.
A heart says, "I love you."
The magic will start,
When you take your first bite
Of a Blueberry Tart!

BREAD PUDDING

BREAD PUDDING

The most boring name
For dessert (no excuse).
Is Bread Pudding. Please stop it.
Don't let it run loose.

For "bread," just say "bun,"
Or something more clever.
For "pudding," say "custard,"
Or simply - whatever -

You know in your heart
You'll return to the first.
You'll still call it Bread Pudding,
Though that isn't the worst!

Carrot Cake

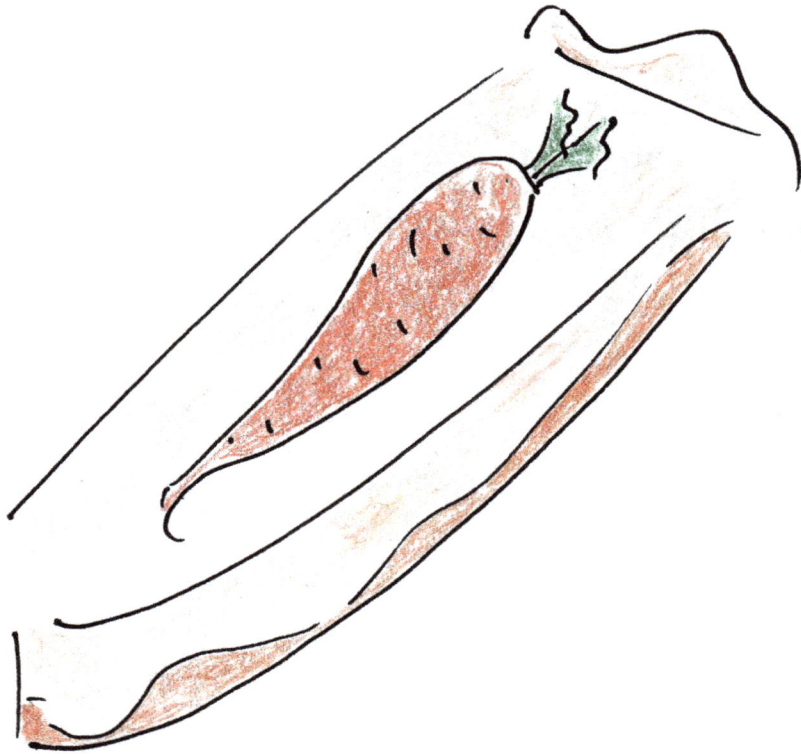

CARROT CAKE

What do you feed
A hungry parrot?
A big slice of Cake,
And please make it Carrot!

Of course, it must have
A petal-pink frosting.
Just simply ignore
How much it is costing!

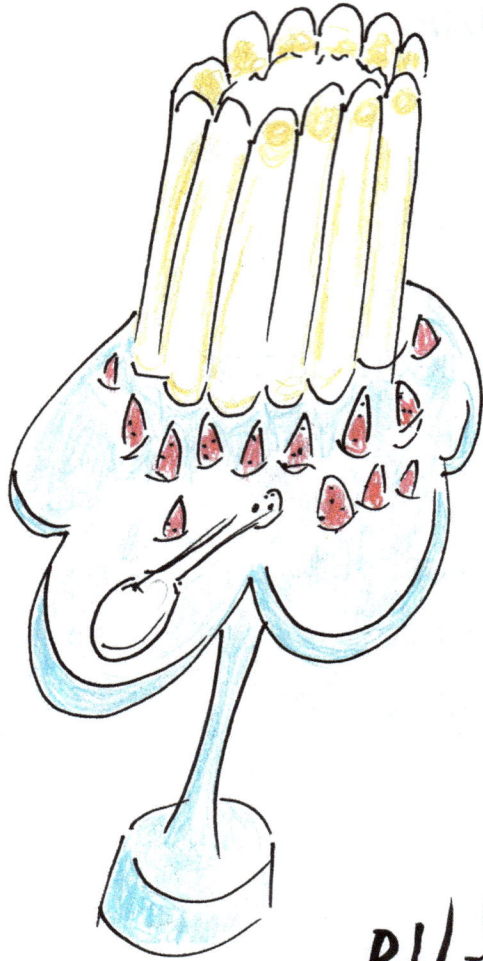

CHARLOTTE RUSSE

CHARLOTTE RUSSE

May I please introduce you
To Miss Charlotte Russe?
In a lovers' triangle
She's the hypotenuse.

She's a glamourous dish
From the mid-19th century.
She takes pride in her taste
Which is always adventury.

CHERRIES JUBILEE

A sight that everyone
Wishes to see,
Are flaming
Cherries Jubilee.

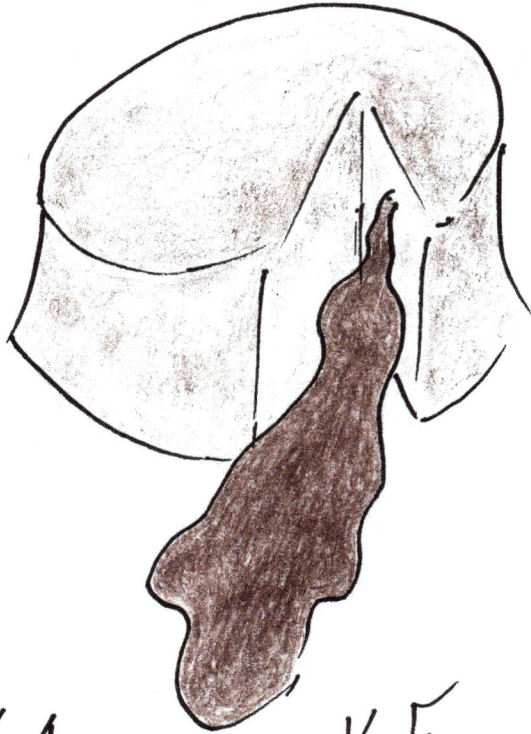

CHOCOLATE

LAVA CAKE

CHOCOLATE LAVA CAKE

I really must have a
Chocolate Lava Cake.

Make no mistake,
I want a
Chocolate Lava Cake.
The only thing
To keep me awake
Is a slice of
Chocolate Lava Cake.
I know my hungry heart
Will break,
If I can't have
A bite of
Chocolate Lava Cake!

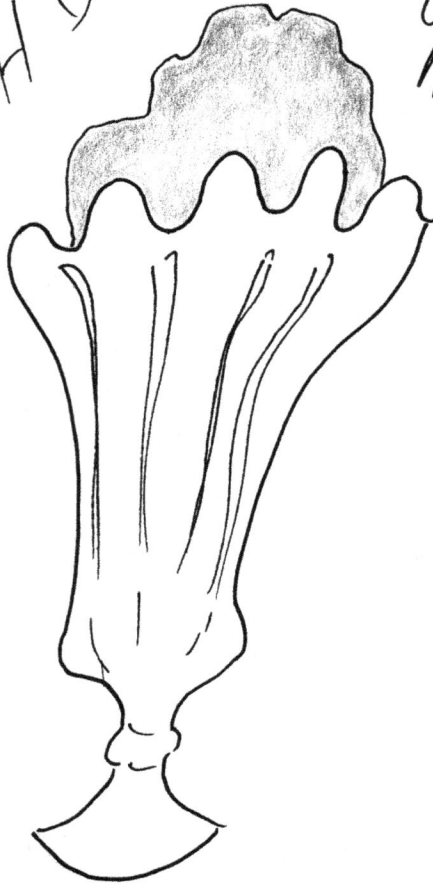

CHOCOLATE Mousse

CHOCOLATE MOUSSE

Did you think Chocolate Mousse was
Chocolate Mouse?
Then you've made a big mistake.
A Chocolate Mousse is a great dessert,
As delicious as Angel Food Cake!

CHOCOLATE
TRUFFLES

CHOCOLATE TRUFFLES

Kick your legs!
Shake your ruffles!
Yes, you can
Cancan!

Celebrate!
It's not too late!
Indulge in
Chocolate Truffles!

NESSELRODE PUDDING

COUNT KARL NESSELRODE'S DESSERTS

Nesselrode Pudding and Nesselrode Pie
Are named for Count Karl,
A great Russian guy.
A statesman, creator of
Puddings and pies,
Food that will cause you
To feast with your eyes.

CRÈME BRÛLÉE

CRÈME BRÛLÉE

Here comes your dessert,
A cold Crème Brûlée,
Like an ice skating rink
For the Queen of the May.

Her tiny feet crackle
The nicely burnt cream.
She skates round the rink
In a heavenly cream.

Is the Queen really real?
What do you think?
Can you now see her skate
On that Crème Brûlée rink?

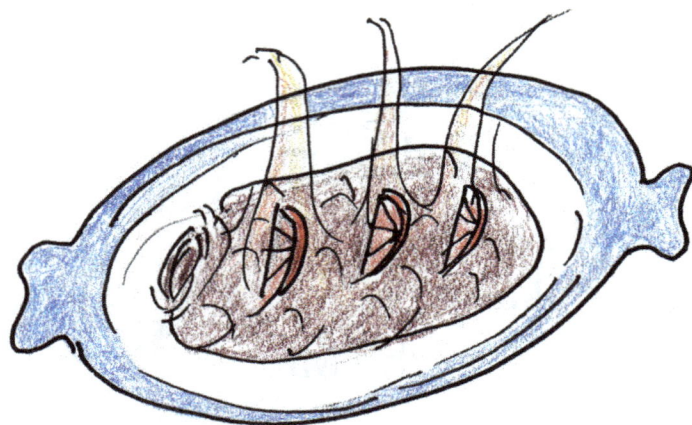

CRÊPÉ
SUZETTE

CRÊPE SUZETTE

A dessert that you always
Begin with a flame,
Has an elegant and always
Enchanting first name.

From a charming French actress,
Suzanne Reichenberg,
Called Suzette, whose real name
I'm sure you'd not heard.

I think she was a notorious flirt,
Bold and saucy,
Young malapert.
Which brings me at last,
To that tasty French treat:
The crêpe that is always
So much fun to eat.

COOKIE BiSCUIT TRISCUIT BUN

DANCING DESSERTS

DANCING DESSERTS

Try to watch a cookie dance,
If you ever get the chance.
Or a warm and buttered biscuit,
Or a tiny tasty Triscuit.
But most of all, just watch a bun
With abundance having fun.

DESSERT
CHEF

DESSERT CHEF

If Rudolf Nureyev,
The ballet dancer,
Were Dessert Chef for the day,
And you asked him in your loudest voice,
"What's for dessert today?"

Here is what he'd say:
"Please lower your voice,
Since I'm not deaf.
And I am also not a chef!
Why not question Oscar Wilde,
Or better yet, Ms. Julia Child?
They could tell you
Right away,
The best dessert we have today.
It's probably old favorite, Crème Brûlée.
Not something dull, like Curds and Whey!

DESSERT FIRST

DESSERT FIRST

Why must we wait
To the end of a meal
To have the best, at last?
By the time the dessert arrives
Your hunger has already passed.

Why not start the meal with
A Crème Brûlée,
A Pear Parfait,
A Flan Flambé,
Or a scrumptious Cherry Tart?
Why not begin the meal
With something great –
That's the perfect way to start.

FLAN

They say that in Spain
They like to eat Flan,
But they order it early
Before it's all gone.

FLAN / SOUFFLÉ

FLAN SOUFFLÉ

Flan served in Japan
Is called "Fl—anne."

Flan served in Bonn
Is called "Fl—ahn."

Flan Soufflé
You can say
Either way.

Floating Island

FLOATING ISLAND

This lovable island
From long, long ago,
Is like no other island
You ever will know.

Most islands will last
A long time, we think,
But dear Floating Island
Always will sink,
Into a very turbulent tummy,
Who thinks Floating Island
Unusually yummy!

A Goose with Gooseberry Mousse

GOOSEBERRY MOUSSE

What kind of a mousse
Would a goose like the best?
Oh, a Gooseberry Mousse
Is what she'd request.

A JELLY ROLL

A JELLY ROLL

Have you
Ever
Watched
A Jelly Roll
Dancing
Up and
Down
A pole?

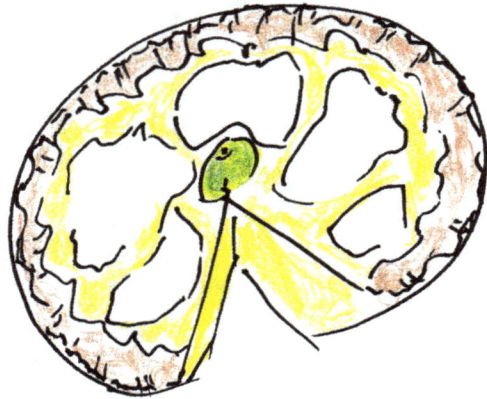

KEY LIME PIE

KEY LIME PIE

Key Limes come from Florida Keys –
Likewise, Key Lime Pies,
Topped by whipped cream or meringue –
A treasure for your eyes!

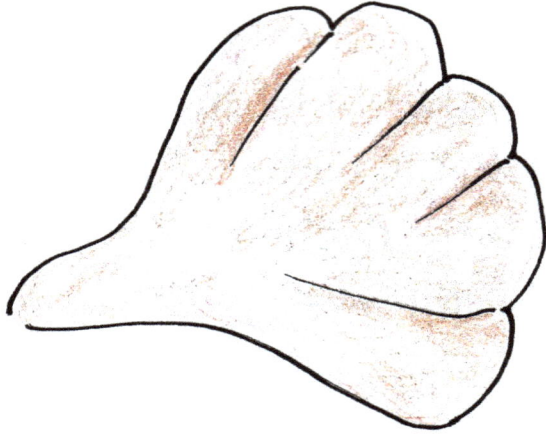

MADELEINE

MADELEINE

A pastry chef named Madeleine
Was a talented mademoiselle.
She designed a delicious pastry
That almost looked like a shell.

Her friends called the pastry "Madeleine,"
In honor of her name.
It could have been called "coquille" or "shell,"
But it's always been called the same:
"Madeleine"

MONT
BLANC

MONT BLANC

Mont Blanc is often hidden
By drifts of whipped cream snow,
Which covers all the slopes,
Where candied violets grow.

PARFAIT

PARFAIT

Parfait is a great dessert
In its tall glass on a stem.
It's a custard with whipped cream and fruit,
And it speaks of our carpe diem.

PETIT
FOURS

PETIT FOURS

Do you remember *The New Yorker*'s
Mary Petty maid?
Prim in her ruffled cap
And forever staid.

We see her serve a tray of
Delicate Petit Fours,
Before she feather-dusts
The gilded pantry doors.

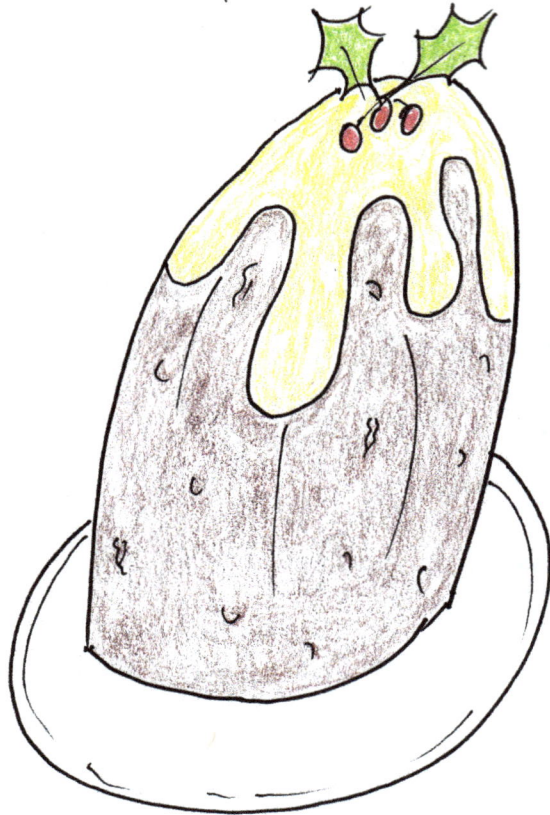

PLUM

PUDDING

PLUM PUDDING: A CURIOUS FACT

No plums in Plum Pudding?
Very strange, but it's true!
Next time you make Plum Pudding,
Please throw in a few!

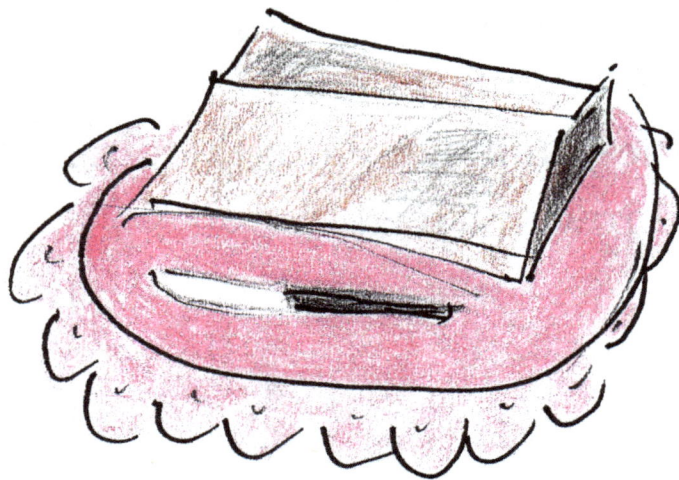

Pound Cake

POUND CAKE

The original Pound Cake recipe
Called for ingredients
By the pound.
A pound of butter, sugar, and flour,
Quite soon the people found
That those who ate this Pound Cake
All gained at least a pound!

PUMPKIN
CHEESECAKE

PUMPKIN CHEESECAKE

Pumpkins star at Halloween.
Cheesecakes star all year.
The two together will inspire
A hungry sonneteer.

RHUBARB
PIE

RHUBARB PIE

Please tell me why
You like plain Rhubarb Pie?
Rhubarb's stringy and dull
Like a gullible gull.

No! No! Rhubarb Pie
Is like pie in the sky.
It is brimming with hope
Like a new Microscope.

It's as sweet as a peach,
Or a day at the beach.
Cheers for great Rhubarb Pie!
A yes-yes and aye-aye!

CRÈME BRÛLÉE

SANTA'S FAVORITE DESSERT

SANTA'S FAVORITE DESSERT

What is more fun at Christmastime,
Than seeing Santa in his sleigh?
Flying over ice and snow
To find at home: a Crème Brûlée.

SHCOFLY

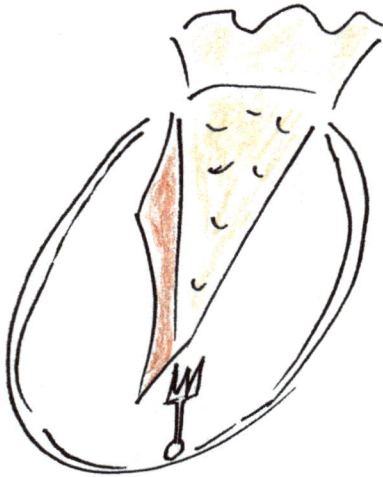

PIE

SHOOFLY PIE

No matter how hard you try,
You'll never shoo a fly
Off a Pennsylvania-Dutch
Brown sugar Shoofly Pie.

SORBET

A SORBET

An ice dessert that we like to be served
Is a colorful Sorbet.
The pink of a rose, the green of a mint,
Or the blue of a sassy blue jay.

SORBET

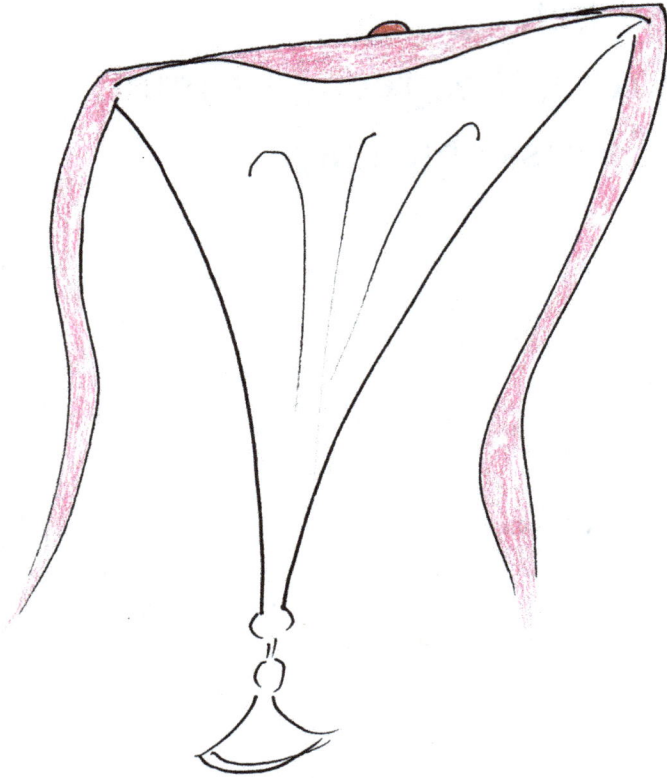

SURPRISE

SORBET SURPRISE

On an elegant menu.
One very hot day,
Came a ritzy dessert:
A Sorbet Flambé.

It was much too expensive.
My mind was a muddle.
When the Sorbet arrived,
It was simply a puddle!

SOUFFLE

GRAND
MARNIER

SOUFFLÉ GRAND MARNIER

For a truly delightful
And super dessert,
Which arouses the taste buds,
And keeps you alert,
Try Soufflé Grand Marnier,
The crème de la crème.
Beloved by both parties:
The Rep. and the Dem.!

STRAWBERRY

SHORTCAKE

STRAWBERRY SHORTCAKE

I hear that you like
Strawberry Shortcake.
Then you really will like
Strawberry Tallcake!

It is covered with
Whipped cream,
Strawberries on top.
As you eat Strawberry Tallcake,
You won't want to stop!

TAPIOCA

Pudding

TAPIOCA

If you wish to dance
The lively carioca,
Try eating a great big spoonsful
Of hot, hot Tapioca.

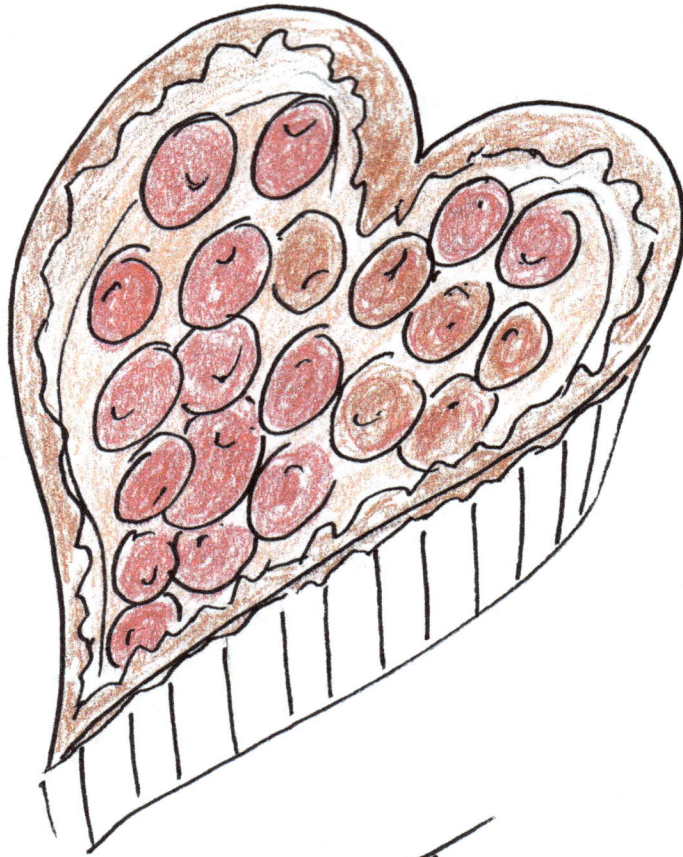

A TART

A TART

A Tart is a tiny and succulent pie.
It's delicious and real, not a pie in the sky.
Make it circular, square, or the shape of a
heart –
So romantic if filled like a French Cherry
Tart.

TIPSY

CAKE

TIPSY CAKE

If a nap you wish to take,
Have a slice of Tipsy Cake.
Then you'll dream you're a dancing Gypsy,
A dream from eating cake called Tipsy.

TiRAMiSU

TIRAMISU

A tear for a dear
For a darling Miss Sue.
She will float in your dreams
Like a chocolate fondue.
Add ladyfingers, espresso,
And dollops of cream.
It will be your indulgent
Decadent dream.

The Trifle

THE TRIFLE

My favorite tower
In all of the world
Is the one in Paris
Called the Eiffel.

My favorite sweet
In England's called
By a trivial name:
The Trifle.

UPSLDE-DOWN CAKE

UPSIDE-DOWN CAKE

We never like things upside-down;
That only makes us nervous.
But mention Upside-Down Cake, and we say,
"Please, the biggest piece you'll serve us!"

About the Author

Rosemary Butler has been sketching ever since she can remember. As a child, trees and buildings were her favorite subjects. She became a fan of the theater, and an art major in college. She designed sets for college and community theaters. Her most prestigious assignment was overseeing the set design for a production of *South Pacific*, at the Kodiak Navy Base in Alaska. Her husband, Charles Butler, was stationed there, and Rosemary was the base librarian. The Alaska Company of *South Pacific* performed to huge crowds in Kodiak, Anchorage, Fairbanks, and the Aleutian Islands.

Now in her nineties, Rosemary continues to enjoy writing collections of light verse and sketching visuals for them. Her previous books include *Ghostly Encounters: Ireland, England, and Spain*, *My Merry Menagerie*, *The Mysterious Snippets of Yarn*, and *Funny Bugs*.

www.ingramcontent.com/pod-product-compliance
Lightning Source LLC
Chambersburg PA
CBHW050639150426
42813CB00054B/1120

* 9 7 8 1 8 8 3 3 7 8 2 5 7 *